▓ THESE BUILDINGS...RESPECT
AN ANCIENT TRADITION. THE
ONLY ONE HERE WORTHY OF
RESPECT—THE PRAIRIE. ▓

—FRANK LLOYD WRIGHT

AUSGEFÜHRTE BAUTEN UND
ENTWÜRFE VON
FRANK LLOYD WRIGHT, 1910

FRANK LLOYD WRIGHT'S
PRAIRIE HOUSES

■■ · C A R L A · · L I N D · ■■

A N   A R C H E T Y P E   P R E S S   B O O K

POMEGRANATE ARTBOOKS, SAN FRANCISCO

Library of Congress Cataloging-in-Publication Data

Lind, Carla.

Frank Lloyd Wright's Prairie houses / Carla Lind.

    p.   cm.

"An Archetype Press book."

Includes bibliographical references.

ISBN 1-56640-997-7

1. Architecture, Domestic—Middle West. 2. Prairie school (Architecture)
3. Wright, Frank Lloyd, 1867–1959—Themes, motives. I. Wright, Frank Lloyd,
1867–1959. II. Title.

NA7218.L56 1994

728'.37'092–dc20

Published by Pomegranate Artbooks

Box 6099, Rohnert Park,

California 94927-6099

Produced by Archetype Press, Inc.

Washington, D.C.

Project Director: Diane Maddex

Art Director: Robert L. Wiser

10 9 8 7 6 5 4 3

Printed in Singapore

94-7924

CIP

Opening photographs: Page 1:
Frank Lloyd Wright about 1908.
Page 2: The barrel-vaulted dining
room of the Dana-Thomas house.

CONTENTS

TYLES, THOUGHT FRANK LLOYD WRIGHT (1867–1959), were narrow definitions that limited creativity and encouraged standardization. To Wright, the only "style" a building had was its inherent character. Rather than *being* a style, it should *have* style. Wright called his work organic architecture because each building grew from within — from the nature of the need, the site, and the materials. From this came its style. Despite the uniqueness of each of his designs, identifiable patterns did develop during various periods of his career. Some of his buildings are called Prairie Style, some textile block, and yet others Usonian because they share distinctive, common features.

The Prairie School of architecture began around the turn of the century. Centered in America's heartland, the Midwest, and based in Chicago, this architectural movement produced a regional style that expressed the spacious, horizontal feeling of the prairies, responded to the region's climate, and was not bound by tradition. Residential architecture was its focus. The theoretical leader of this movement toward an indigenous architecture was Louis Sullivan, a man of principle and vision for whom

The May house (pages 6–7) rests on the north edge of its lot, opening it to the southern sunshine. Inside, art glass geometry (opposite) draws on Wright's early education with the Froebel blocks.

The *Ladies' Home Journal* helped spread the word about Wright's work by publishing three of his basic house plans. This one, for "A Home in a Prairie Town" (1901), had a hipped roof and a cruciform plan in which the living, dining, and library areas were in line. Estimated cost: $6,970.

Wright apprenticed when he was in his early twenties. Wright, however, became the leading and best-known practitioner of the Prairie Style.

The seeds of the Prairie Style were rooted in an appreciation for nature and a dedication to the freedom and individuality inherent in democracy. To that Wright added his own experiences and influences: his mother's teaching, via the Froebel gifts, that natural law could be understood through geometric abstractions; his father's passion for music, which introduced him to composition and harmony;

the literature of the day that informed him about the Aesthetic and Arts and Crafts movements and transcendental writers such as Whitman, Emerson, and Thoreau, who encouraged an honest, nature-inspired life; the Japanese art and architecture at the World's Columbian Exposition, which exemplified simplicity. From these arose a common theme of unity, harmony, simplicity, and respect for the nature of materials and the uniqueness of the individual. These were ideals in which midwesterners believed. For fourteen years Wright experimented, searching for a

unified expression of his beliefs. Finally, in 1900, came a synthesis. The Prairie Style blossomed from this fertile ground.

About twenty other architects are identified with the movement. Most of their activity centered around Wright's Oak Park studio until it closed in 1910, after he departed for Europe. The Prairie Style continued to be practiced until a few years after World War I, when it was overwhelmed by interest in colonial and revival styles.

Thanks to a steady stream of adventurous, confident clients, this was one of Wright's most prolific periods. In one decade he designed three hundred buildings, 119 of which were built. Using the grammar and rationale of organic architecture, Wright was able to create diverse compositions because each was a unified, integrated response to the individuality of both the client and the site. While only a few Prairie Style designs were built in the 1920s and 1930s, some of Wright's work as late as 1950 reflects his Prairie School heritage. Revolutionary and productive, the Prairie period was just one early chapter in Wright's architectural career—an epic that did not conclude for another fifty years.

Dominant horizontal lines

Low hipped, gabled, or flat roofs with wide overhangs. Broad, low chimneys

Open plans

Fewer and more open, less boxlike rooms

Simplified spaces

Primary living spaces raised to the second floor for privacy and grander vistas. Basements and attics often eliminated

Human scale

Reduced ceiling heights and wood bands and decks that lower perceived heights

Integral ornament

Limited and integrated ornament, the result of artful manipulation of building materials rather than pieces attached to a building

Geometric plans

Angular (primarily rectangular) shapes for plans and details

Integrated windows and doors

Ribbon windows like light screens, opposing solid walls. Generous art glass windows and skylights

Integrated elements

All aspects designed as part of the integrated whole, including built-in furniture and carefully selected decorative objects

Organic siting

Buildings that appear to grow from their sites, connected to the landscape with terraces, outreaching garden walls, planters, and urns

Natural materials

Treatments that reveal the nature of the materials. Wood stained or clear coated, never painted. Wood bands and balusters cut straight, not forced into curly shapes. Plaster walls often stained or stippled to reduce their solidity but no wallpaper. Stucco and rough-sawn wood used but only rarely stone

Prominent hearth

Fireplaces that serve as a home's architectural and sociological heart

Individuality

Designs that reflect the needs of the clients

Top: The prairielike layers of the Robie house and a massive hearth at the Darwin Martin house. Bottom: Sparkling art glass windows by a skylight as well as flowing spaces at the May house.

Unified elements

All interior features designed as part of a harmonious whole

Geometric design motifs

Simple stylized forms used as the basis of all components, many derived from plants and flowers

Natural colors

Palettes drawn from the woods and prairies, especially the colors of autumn: golds, browns, rusty oranges, and yellow-greens

Built-in furniture

Rectilinear pieces—cabinets, seating, shelves, radiators—built in using the materials, details, scale, and colors of the house itself

Freestanding furniture

Chairs, settles, and tables created as floating parts of the structure

Focus on dining rooms

Tall-back chairs, special lighting (often part of the table), and intimate arrangements emphasizing the significance of the occasion

Recessed light fixtures

Patterned grilles with geometric patterns that recreate nature's filtered and reflected light. Wooden light decks to cast soft shadows

Natural accessories

Flowers, weeds, tree branches, evergreens, and grasses informally arranged

Intricate windows

Geometrically patterned art glass windows that act as light screens. Few draperies, although some portières used in doorways to control drafts

Coordinated floor coverings

Custom-designed carpets that repeat the motifs and colors of the space. Oriental and native American rugs added for accent

Natural textiles

Natural materials such as linen, cotton, and wool in flat weaves or velvets and leather for chairs. Coordinated table and bed linens

Simplified artworks

Murals, Japanese screens, and sculptures integrated with the architecture, but no hanging pictures

Details from the Dana-Thomas house: Butterfly art glass over the entry, a fountain sculpture in the reception area, a spindle-back chair and table, and a double-pedestal art glass lamp.

BRADLEY HOUSE (GLENLLOYD)

KANKAKEE, ILLINOIS. 1900

☷ Few architects have given us more poetic translations of material into structure than Frank Lloyd Wright. ☷
Robert C. Spencer, Jr.
Architectural Review, 1900

The broad, polygonal bay of the Bradley house provides open, well-lighted spaces on both the first and the second floors. Angular art glass windows take their design cue from the roof's shallow gables. The long bands of art glass windows are mostly clear, with small touches of red and white.

MRS. HARLEY BRADLEY AND HER brother Warren Hickox inherited a beautiful wooded site along the Kankakee River where each built a home designed by Wright. The more elaborate of the two, the Bradley house is an example of the "Small House with 'Lots of Room in It,'" one of Wright's basic plans published in the *Ladies' Home Journal* in 1901. Hardly small, it was 6,000 square feet.

Beneath the low, gabled, cedar-shingled roofs stretch simple planes of tan stucco and bands of geometric art glass neatly tied together with ribbons of rough-sawn cocoa-stained wood. The casement windows, when grouped, became light screens rather than simple holes to let light inside. The pinwheel plan is revealed on entering from the side carriage entrance. Rooms reach outside through polygonal bay windows, onto terraces or verandas—dissolving the box and increasing the sense of space by borrowing from the natural world beyond.

Despite the building's suitability as a home, the site and generous spaces seem to invite nonresidential use. For many years it was used as a restaurant and now, after restoration, it houses offices.

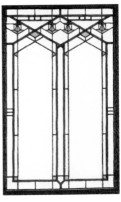

Wright designed freestanding and built-in furniture for the Bradley house, as well as art glass, carpets, and lighting— all part of the unified whole.

WILLITS HOUSE

AN AMPLE WOODED LOT COMBINED with the right clients at the right time inspired Wright to create what he called his "first great Prairie house." It was a handsome but not ostentatious shelter for a prominent family who shared Wright's love for the Japanese aesthetic of simplicity. In 1905 Frank and Catherine Wright made their first visit to Japan with Ward and Cecilia Willits.

Similar to his *Ladies' Home Journal* plan published the same year, the Willits house revealed all the classic features of the style. Throughout the interior, an over-lapping of walls and partial walls—like Japanese sliding screens—allows a blend of glimpses and vistas inviting in-vestigation. Believing that the space within the building was more important than its enclosure, Wright sought to open the box. Windows were an important tool. He placed them at corners where piers used to be. He grouped them along walls to destroy the solidity. He connected them to other planes with simple wood moldings.

Here, the harmonious order yielded an eloquent model of simplicity—every facet influenced by Wright's childhood education with the geometric Froebel blocks.

⊞ The endless adaptability of the Prairie House formula was perhaps its greatest miracle. ⊞
Grant Carpenter Manson
Frank Lloyd Wright to 1910, 1958

The gregarious dining room, a peninsula with art glass on three sides and above, makes the living room, with its low horizontal form, seem intimate. The rectilinear furniture pieces are variations on the general design motifs of the house itself.

The staircase opens to an
art glass skylight, offering
a dramatic interplay of
screens, planes, and
volumes. The house's
complex plan combined a
pinwheel and a cruciform.
Its light stucco walls are
boldly delineated with
dark wood bands, wrap-
ping around corners—
ignoring them.

FRICKE HOUSE

ONE OF WRIGHT'S MANY 1901 COMMISSIONS, the house of William Fricke (also known as the Emma Martin house) is somewhat of a paradox. It is decidedly vertical, culminating in a third-story billiard room, yet it is powerfully horizontal in its feeling. The long, low lines of the hipped roof are accentuated by the wood trim on the exterior, which connects windows and defines planes. The nearly cubist simplicity of the rectilinear stucco masses is broken by the triangular projections from the reception room and the east bedroom.

The entrance, off to one side, is gradual, enclosing visitors more and more until they are inside. Then they are released into free-flowing spaces. The interior confirms the dominance of the horizontal and the rectangle. The living room and dining room rest back-to-back around the fireplace—simple wood banding wrapping the walls, skimming the ceiling, bringing all spaces into the whole.

By placing the home on the north edge of the lot, a favored Wright technique, he made the site seem larger and invited the warm, southern sunlight into this northern home.

The Fricke house was one of the few commissions Wright did during a brief partnership with Webster Tomlinson. The interplay of line and plane in the stairhall (opposite) is dramatic.

The verticality of the form (pages 28–29) and the minicolumns between the windows are reminiscent of Wright's earlier Heller and Husser residences and bear Louis Sullivan's influence. Unfortunately, an attached garden house was demolished and its lot rebuilt. The garage, the first in the Prairie Style, still stands.

DANA-THOMAS HOUSE

SPRINGFIELD, ILLINOIS. 1902

Decorative elements enrich the house. A terra-cotta frieze (above and pages 32–33) wraps the exterior. The gallery (opposite) has some of the hundreds of custom-designed decorative arts.

THE YOUNG ARCHITECT WAS COMMISSIONED to build his first truly grand residence by Susan Lawrence Dana, a socially and politically prominent heiress. She wanted a spacious and impressive house suitable for entertaining but required that Wright build it around the family's Italianate home. The result was a magical masterpiece of geometric forms enriched with intricate detail— swallowing all but a small library of the original residence.

The bold geometry of the 12,500-square-foot house is introduced by the arched entrance in the imposing tawny brick facade. Above the door, a "butterfly wreath" of golden art glass admits a glow into the foyer, from which stairs rise to the principal rooms. Inside, the geometry becomes three-dimensional as the rooms change levels and varying volumes of space invite easy circulation and exploration of extravagantly ornamented rooms. The sunny autumn color scheme sparkles through screens of glass, partially revealing spaces ahead.

The drama of the spaces has been faithfully restored by the state of Illinois in recognition of the lasting importance of this work of art drawn from the prairie.

HEURTLEY HOUSE

■■ The Prairie School could not have existed without a certain concurrence of objectives and ideals between the architects and their clients. ■■

H. Allen Brooks
Frank Lloyd Wright and the Prairie School, 1984

DOWN THE STREET FROM HIS OWN home, Wright designed the restrained Heurtley house. It is a composed statement of simple shelter on a flat suburban grid. Rather than a cruciform, it is a square plan, which has been stretched into a rectangle by the covered porch. Beneath the shallow hipped roof rise Roman brick walls, so carefully detailed that periodic courses of a lighter color protrude, creating a horizontal rhythm that exemplifies Wright's use of integral ornament. The outstretched arms of the garden walls and even the low, wide chimney further help engage the building with the earth. The extended bands of art glass windows beneath the eaves seem to lift the roof off the walls and float it above.

A triangular projection with a circular urn marks the entry. To reach the main living quarters on the second floor, one climbs a stair tunnel. At the top lies the open stretch of living and dining spaces. The living room ceiling is pitched like a tent, with art glass skylights over the arched fireplace. Seated at the piano or the dining table, the music-loving Arthur Heurtley could enjoy the activity on the street below from the privacy of his shelter.

The entry to the Heurtley house is a massive, cavelike arch sheltered under a broad, protective roof that mirrors the lines of the prairie.

The arched entrance form is echoed in the living room fireplace, which dominates the space. The triangular forms of the skylight overhead repeat the wall projections, express the overhanging roofline, and energize the entire design.

DARWIN MARTIN HOUSE

DARWIN MARTIN. AN EXECUTIVE WITH THE Larkin Company in Buffalo, met Wright at the recommendation of his brother William, who was already a Wright client. Wright eventually gained nine commissions and a loyal patron from this pivotal connection.

Early visitors would look down a long pergola to the conservatory (both now demolished)—an expansive and memorable view. The huge living room, dining room, library, and porch are separated only by piers, not walls. Art glass screens and bands of windows open spaces even further to five porches and verandas. To the left of the hall is a reception room with an elegant arched fireplace, an office, the kitchen, and service areas. The staircase rises to eight bedrooms and a sewing room and descends to a large playroom in the basement. Countless nature-based art glass windows and skylights as well as metallic gold mortar joints lighten and complement the composition as leaves and blossoms glorify sturdy tree trunks.

The state of New York and the University of New York at Buffalo have recently agreed to pursue the restoration of this Wright masterwork.

⊞ The Prairie houses are each a study in the flow of space, from the intimacy of the entry to the open excitement of the main rooms. ⊞

Brian A. Spencer
The Prairie School Tradition,
1979

Long, shallow, hipped roofs and broad chimneys mark the cross axes of the elaborate T plan of the 10,000-square-foot structure. Verticals and horizontals are masterfully interwoven throughout. The entrance is hidden from view beneath a protective porte-cochère.

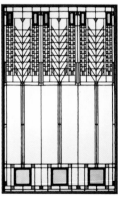

The horizontal light decks
and wood banding connect
vast spaces, providing a
human scale. Many of the
windows have been removed.

ROBIE HOUSE

FOR INVENTOR AND BUSINESSMAN Frederick C. Robie, Wright engineered a streamlined city house that now epitomizes the Prairie Style. The massive masonry structure nearly fills its city lot, enclosing the garden and what may be Wright's first attached garage.

Inside, levels change but the horizontal feel continues. The primary living spaces are on the second level, open to the outside through long bands of windows deeply recessed to allow privacy from the busy city street. Both the living room, on one side of the fireplace, and the dining room, on the other, end in triangular bays, one of Wright's common techniques for releasing the box. The triangular patterns in the art glass mimic the rooflines, repeating the shape. Concealed steel beams are cantilevered to create long, uninterrupted spaces that continue through windows out onto porches and balconies, the walls nearly nonexistent. The bedrooms are secluded on the third level.

The furniture, supervised by George Niedecken, is as much a part of the architecture as the structure—all components of the same unified environment.

⚏ In this house one completely feels the spirit of our age. . . . One thinks of an automobile, rather than a horse-drawn carriage, as being appropriate for this home. ⚏

J. J. P. Oud, architect, 1918

The furniture was so extensive that it added $10,000 to the cost of the $50,000 house. Simple red oak was used for the rectilinear forms that served as tables, chairs, and cabinets. The most elaborate of these was the dining room table with built-in light fixtures. Surrounded by tall chairs, it became a lighted sculpture for dining — private and dramatic.

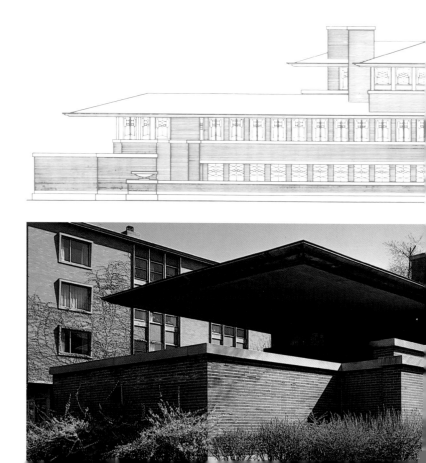

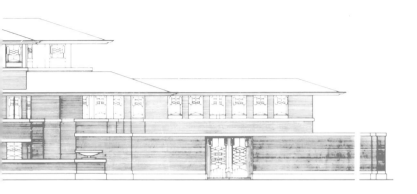

The three-story height of the house, now owned by the University of Chicago, is subdued by the strength of long, low layers of red-tiled, hipped roofs. They are arranged in an abstract composition of horizontal forms accented by occasional vertical elements.

COONLEY HOUSE

All furnishings (opposite) were variations on the general motifs of the house, becoming interlocking parts of a harmonious, poetic whole.

With its numerous planters and reflective pools, the garden (page 48) contributes to the magic of the design. Tiny colored tiles, geometric art glass designs, and patterned copper eaves (page 49) enrich the low, sandy stucco walls beneath red tile roofs.

THE COONLEYS WERE PROGRESSIVE and trusting clients who provided Wright a wooded site along the Des Plaines River and a generous budget. They were rewarded with an imaginative, intricately articulated, grand pavilion for living.

All rooms except a playroom are on the second floor, grouped into activity zones. The driveway pierces the composition as it moves beneath the second floor, confirming the feeling of a raised platform. Complex, integral ornament becomes part of the house's three-dimensional, geometric puzzle. Repeated throughout is the central design theme—the square and the rectangle.

The exterior shape of the house is expressed in the sloping ceiling of the living room, which has an intricate composition of wood banding punctuated with patterned grilles over indirect light and art glass skylights. This filters the light shed on a mural of a birch woods and the overall autumnal color scheme, creating the restful feeling of a forest glen. Long bands of nature-inspired art glass frame the views of the riverway beyond. Wright virtually dematerialized the walls.

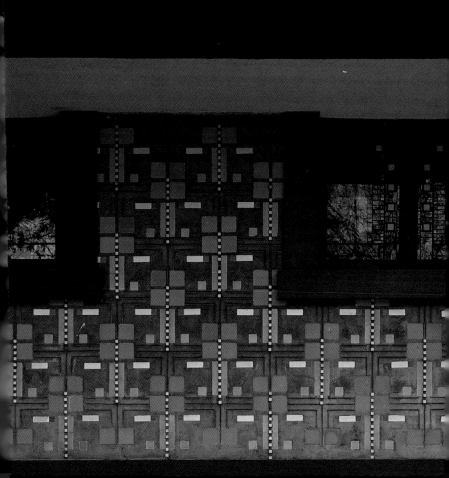

STOCKMAN HOUSE

MASON CITY, IOWA. 1908

▓▓ It opens, we enter, and an atmosphere of quiet strength and well-ordered repose envelops us, refreshes us, and gives us confidence in the personality of the "owners," assures us of depth, warmth and simplicity. ▓▓

Frank Lloyd Wright
Architect, Architecture and Client, 1896

The living and dining rooms are placed in an ell around the fireplace. Wood banding and decks overhead serve to lead the eye from room to room and provide the illusion of greater space.

A REMINDER OF WRIGHT'S LIFE-long desire to make good architecture available to middle-class families, the Stockman house is an excellent example of his design for "A Fireproof House for $5,000" published in the *Ladies' Home Journal* in 1907. The prototype had a flat roof and was meant to be built of poured concrete like Unity Temple so that it would be affordable for the average American. The simple cube had windows grouped in bands and a protected entry on one side.

Wright's design for Dr. and Mrs. George C. Stockman deviated in that it had a hipped roof, was stucco with wood banding, and had a covered veranda off the living and dining rooms that stretched the square into a more horizontal form. It represents a variation on an efficient and inexpensive design that was copied by other Prairie School architects and became a vernacular style.

The only example in Iowa of Wright's Prairie Style, the house was scheduled for demolition in 1990. The community mobilized but was forced to move it to a new site. Now it sits happily in a Prairie School enclave and is operated by the River City Society for Historic Preservation.

MAY HOUSE

FOR MEYER MAY, A RESPECTED HABERDASHER, Wright designed a golden jewel box for a flat, narrow lot. While it is not grand in scale, it beautifully illustrates many typical Prairie Style features. Beneath the shallow hipped roof and wide overhangs are graceful walls of tan brick broken by bands of geometric art glass casements. To maximize the benefits of the southern exposure, Wright placed the house to the far north side of the lot and then opened it generously to the south. Exotic patterns of copper wrap around the living room windows, adding drama to the geometry. Nestled more than a foot below grade, embracing the site, the cruciform plan deviates from many of Wright's Prairie designs.

The living and dining rooms are separated not by a fireplace, which is placed on an outside wall, but by a hallway with a floral mural on one side and a spindle screen on the other, both of which seem to dissolve the partitions. Light fixtures and even embroidered linens were designed as part of the unified whole. Sixteen original carpets were recreated as part of the comprehensive restoration completed by Steelcase Inc. in 1987.

⌗ Our first impression is our truest; it is overwhelming, a consummate work of art, powerful and complete, far beyond anything we have a right to expect in a small house. ⌗
Vincent Scully
The Meyer May House, 1987

Because the furnishings were supervised by George Niedecken simultaneously with the Robie house, the two houses have many features in common. Some of the furniture designs are the same and others are similar, most notably the dining room table with high-back chairs and built-in light fixtures.

A golden color scheme
begins with ample oak trim,
moves to stippled wall
finishes, covers the uphol-
stered furniture, and glistens
in the golden glass placed in
the fireplace mortar joints,
skylights, and windows.

FURTHER READING

Brooks, H. Allen. *Frank Lloyd Wright and the Prairie School.* New York: George Braziller, 1984.

―――. *The Prairie School: Frank Lloyd Wright and His Midwest Contemporaries.* 1972. New York: W. W. Norton, 1976.

Hitchcock, Henry-Russell. *In the Nature of Materials: The Buildings of Frank Lloyd Wright, 1887–1941.* 1942. Reprint. New York: Da Capo Press, 1969.

Manson, Grant Carpenter. *Frank Lloyd Wright to 1910: The First Golden Age.* New York: Van Nostrand Reinhold, 1958.

Pfeiffer, Bruce Brooks, ed. *Frank Lloyd Wright Monographs.* Vols. 1, 2, 3. Tokyo: ADA Edita, 1987.

―――. *Frank Lloyd Wright Selected Houses.* Vol. 1. Tokyo: ADA Edita, 1991.

Wright, Frank Lloyd. *Drawings and Plans of Frank Lloyd Wright: The Early Period (1893–1909).* 1910. Reprint. New York: Dover Publications, 1983.

―――. *The Early Work of Frank Lloyd Wright: The "Ausgeführte Bauten" of 1911.* Reprint. New York: Dover Publications, 1982.

ACKNOWLEDGMENTS

The author wishes to thank the Frank Lloyd Wright Home and Studio Foundation Research Center, the Oak Park Public Library, and especially the generous owners of the houses included here. Special appreciation is due David Christiansen, Jan and William Dring, Jack Prost, Mr. and Mrs. Milt Robinson, and Mr. and Mrs. Nick Sahlas for their assistance with new photography.

Archetype Press is grateful to Balthazar Korab for his assistance with the cover illustration by Robert L. Wiser.

Illustration Sources:

Art Institute of Chicago, Ryerson and Burnham Libraries: 48

Ausgeführte Bauten und Entwürfe von Frank Lloyd Wright (Wasmuth, 1910): 10–11, 12, 18, 20, 35, 46, 47

© Judith Bromley: 23, 24–25, 26, 36–37, 49; courtesy Dana-Thomas house: 2, 16 top left and right, 16 bottom left, 30, 31, 32–33; courtesy Robie House at the University of Chicago: 42

Doug Carr, courtesy Dana-Thomas House: 16 bottom right

Frank Lloyd Wright Home and Studio Foundation: 1 (H&S 277)

Biff Henrich, 39, 41

Historic American Buildings Survey: 43, 44–45 top

Balthazar Korab Ltd.: 15 top left and bottom left, 28–29, 34, 44–45 bottom

K. C. Kratt: 15 top right, 40

Metropolitan Museum of Art: 21 (1983.514)

Ronald Moline, FAIA: 19

Matt Phalen, River City Society for Historic Preservation: 50

Steelcase Inc.: 6–7, 8, 15 bottom right, 53, 54–55

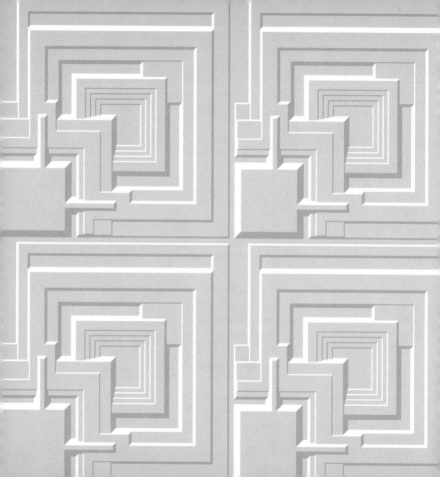